Wolfgang Amadeus Mozart

# THE IMPRESARIO

(Der Schauspieldirektor)

A Comedy with Music in One Act

Libretto by
### STEPHANIE THE YOUNGER

Music by
## W. A. MOZART

English Adaptation by
GIOVANNI CARDELLI

Ed.2108

## G. SCHIRMER, Inc.

DISTRIBUTED BY

7777 W. BLUEMOUND RD. P.O. BOX 13819 MILWAUKEE, WI 53213

## NOTE

## DRAMATIS PERSONAE

MR. SCRUPLES, the old-school Impresario....................Spoken

MR. BLUFF, his assistant................................Baritone

MR. ANGEL, an elderly stage-struck financier....................Tenor

MADAME GOLDENTRILL, an aging opera star..............Soprano

MISS SILVERPEAL, an aspirant opera star..................Soprano

The scene is Mr. Scruples' office in Salzburg, late 18th century

Duration of Performance:
Approximately 55 minutes

*This adaptation dedicated to the memory of Albert Spalding*

Mozart composed this little "Singspiel" in 1786, to a libretto by Stephanie the Younger, author of the book for *Die Entführung aus dem Serail*. The first performance took place in the Orangerie, at Schönbrunn, during an entertainment given by the Emperor Joseph II for the Governor General of the Netherlands. Mozart's spirited jest at the problems of an opera manager's life shared the billing with a satire on Italian opera by the composer's contemporary, Antonio Salieri, 'Prima la musica, e poi le parole'. (*The music first, the words after.*)

In the cast of the première were Stephanie the Younger as the Impresario; Joseph Lange, Mozart's brother-in-law and portraitist, as Bluff; Mozart's sister-in-law, Aloysia Lange, as Madame Goldentrill, and the celebrated Catarina Cavalieri, who created the role of Constanza in *The Seraglio*, as Miss Silverpeal.

The admittedly weak and sprawling libretto has been the object of repeated revisions designed to strengthen the fragile framework on which the incomparable Mozart hung such gems as the Overture, the disputatious Trio and the closing Vaudeville.

In the present version, the original cast of ten, six of whom never sing, has been reduced to five, thus eliminating the lengthy and irrelevant dramatic auditions which have no connection with the music. This has also lead to a material reduction in the length of the purely spoken material.

The mock pathos of the two soprano arias has been retained, together with their tongue-in-cheek solemnity, so deftly reminiscent of the same composer's tragic heroines. The acrimonious pyrotechnics in which the two prima donnas strive for top billing is paraphrased from the original, and the lofty note sounded in the finale, a most haunting echo of *The Seraglio's* "Wer so viel Huld vergessen kann", has been underlined by what appears a logical dénouement to the scrupulous Impresario's dilemma.

G. C.

# The Impresario
## Der Schauspieldirektor

Stephanie the Younger
English adaptation by
Giovanni Cardelli

Wolfgang Amadeus Mozart
K. 486

### Overture

Presto

43108c

4

43108

# THE IMPRESSARIO

*(As the curtain rises, we see the rather shabby office of the Impresario, Mr. Scruples, who is at his desk, gazing out of the window with a far away, discouraged air. Shortly after the rise of the curtain, the door flies open to admit Mr. Bluff, Mr. Scruples' enthusiastic, but rather bumbling assistant; he is greatly excited.)*

## Scene 1

*(Scruples and Bluff)*

**Bluff:** At last! I have it! Mr. Scruples, the contract has been signed naming you Impresario and General Manager of the Court Theater for the coming season!

**Scruples:** I don't believe it! Anyway, it is too late! I have made up my mind to retire to the country and farm.

**Bluff:** Mr. Scruples! I expected you to be so happy!

**Scruples:** Happy? My application has been subjected to such endless delays that my cash, my credit, my enthusiasm, and my patience are exhausted! I am sick and tired of all the intrigues and jealousies that plague an Impresario! I repeat: I am turning farmer!

**Bluff:** Don't I know how you feel? I too have known frustration; and, if you will only let me sing a few well chosen roles, I will gladly shoulder all your burdens!

**Scruples:** My dear Bluff! You're a good fellow, but we have been all through this before; if I were to allow you to sing, the public would butcher us both! Besides, I have in mind a season of classical drama which, God be praised, requires no singers.

**Bluff:** But, Mr. Scruples, the Minister of Education has decreed that the season must be entirely devoted to opera!

**Scruples:** Opera? A ridiculous Italian disease that won't last!

**Bluff:** How can you say such a thing, Mr. Scruples?

**Scruples:** Opera involves too much extravagant expense.

**Bluff:** Mr. Scruples, that may have been true thirty years ago, but today opera can be produced quite economically!

**Scruples:** What about all the singers which opera requires?

**Bluff:** The up-to-date Impresario engages only three kinds! Falling stars, whose fees have shrunk with their range; the public will accept anything from a famous name.

**Scruples:** That is one kind!

**Bluff:** Then some beginners whose obvious shortcomings will be to your credit, since you will be giving native talent a patriotic chance. You pay them nothing.

**Scruples:** I suppose the third group pays me?

**Bluff:** Naturally; these are the ones more blessed with the goods of this world than with talent or voice!

**Scruples:** So that, actually, the low fees of your fallen stars will be paid by the rich amateurs? The singers will cost me nothing?

**Bluff:** On the contrary, Mr. Scruples, they should bring you in a handsome profit!

**Scruples:** My dear Bluff! What kind of operas could one mount with singers recruited by such distasteful, not to say dishonest, means?

**Bluff:** The very best! Those authentic masterpieces which require more acting of a singer than singing!

**Scruples:** What about the costumes, the scenery, the lighting, the mob scenes?

**Bluff:** Nothing simpler? Announce that you are going to modernize opera. To achieve a sense of intimate communication, you eliminate mob scenes!

**Scruples:** A splendid way to shorten a lengthy work!

**Bluff:** To highlight the hidden meanings and the introspective conflicts, we dispense with scenery and play everything before black drapes!

**Scruples:** That eliminates the designer and the painters!

**Bluff:** And most of the stagehands! To promote the utmost realism, we play in modern dress; no costumes!

**Scruples:** And no legs!

**Bluff:** And to intensify the atmospheric moods, we will use very little light; this is very desirable for most singers and will save a pretty penny each week in wax candles! What do you say to these ideas, Mr. Scruples?

**Scruples:** I say that they are deeply repugnant to everything I have always believed in and fought for in the theater. Decidedly, I prefer to be a farmer than to become a party to such an utter degradation of good taste!

**Bluff:** But Mr. Scruples! Good taste is just an expression forever on the lips of those who can not bring themselves to swallow it!

**Scruples:** Are you seriously suggesting that I should stoop to buying success?

**Bluff:** Is there a surer way? Oh, Mr. Scruples, if you had seen what my father had to go through to make his restaurant pay, you would realize that you can only afford to list foie gras and truffles on your bill of fare as long as your kitchen is turning out sausages and sauerkraut!

**Scruples:** My poor Bluff, you yourself don't believe half of what you say! If you were really the rascal you sound like, I would urge you to forget your singing, which you should do anyway, and take over my position, though not my name.

**Bluff:** Oh, thank you, Mr. Scruples; but I am really an artist at heart and I feel that I could serve you best on the stage. You don't agree? I see you don't!

**Scruples:** Cheer up, Bluff, since it doesn't make the slightest difference what either of us think; we have not even enough credit left to print the tickets, let alone undertake a season.

**Bluff:** I know things look very dark, Mr. Scruples, but there is a potential dawn just outside; Mr. Angel has been waiting to see you for the past quarter of an hour.

**Scruples:** Mr. Angel? The Viennese banker? That stage-struck haunter of soprano dressing rooms! What does he want?

**Bluff:** I can guess! He was at the Ministry when your license was issued and he came over to see you at once. I'll show him in; but please, Mr. Scruples, don't be too hasty!

*(Bluff ignores Scruples' gesture of refusal and goes to the door where he bows low to admit the pompous elderly banker, Mr. Angel.)*

## Scene 2

*(Scruples, Bluff and Angel)*

**Angel:** My dear Director! Salzburg is indeed fortunate in its choice of an Impresario! I rather envy you, you know!

**Scruples:** I don't see why you should, but thank you just the same.

**Angel:** Because it happens that I need your help; and, if I were you, I could simply help myself! Ha, ha!

**Scruples:** Ah, ah! But what can I do for you, Mr. Angel?

**Angel:** Quite a lot, Mr. Scruples; quite a lot! between men of the world, and of business, such as ourselves, preliminaries are a waste of time. So, I'll come to the point!

**Bluff:** Mr. Scruples, Mr. Angel is coming to the point!

**Scruples:** Thank you, Bluff; pray do, Mr. Angel.

*(During the following, Scruples tries hard, but in vain, to repress Bluff's excited desire to break into the discussion.)*

**Angel:** You are probably aware that for some time I have maintained a close relationship with one of the lyric stage's brightest ornaments, Madame Goldentrill?

**Scruples:** *The* Madame Goldentrill? Such singers are not heard anymore; truly magnificent! I remember her debut in Budapest, thirty years ago. She recently retired, I believe?

**Angel:** Yes, and no, if you take my meaning. Confidentially, I had hoped that the amenities which I have been privileged to provide would help her forget the stage. But Madame apparently misses the excitement and she is determined to make a whole series of farewell performances.

**Scruples:** I see; and she would like to appear with this company?

**Angel:** Mr. Scruples, it is a pleasure to converse with such a perceptive man. You should have been in business! To be candid, my life with Madame will not be worth living unless you engage her. It would be worth a great deal to me, I can assure you.

**Scruples:** The truth is . . . that problems . . . of repertoire . . .

**Bluff:** What Mr. Scruples means, Mr. Angel, is that the repertoire in which Madame Goldentrill would naturally wish to appear is beyond the resources of our company.

**Angel:**     But I said it would be worth a great deal to me; ten thousand crowns, to be precise! Of course, Mr. Scruples, Madame realizes that it must be some time since you have heard her and that malicious tongues are never idle, so she is prepared to audition for you and is, in fact, waiting in her carriage. I shall go and fetch her!

**Scruples:**     I am afraid that . . .

**Bluff:**     What Mr. Scruples means, Mr. Angel, is that this room is hardly suitable acoustically for an artist of Madame Goldentrill's exceptional vocal power. However, if Madame will overlook this inconvenience, Mr. Scruples will be happy to hear her and renew a precious friendship!

*(Bluff hurriedly ushers Mr. Angel out before Scruples can register an effective protest.)*


Scene 3


*(Scruples and Bluff)*

**Scruples:**     Are you insane? Never in my life have I accepted money from a singer; and I don't propose to start now!

**Bluff:**     Please, do not be angry, Mr. Scruples! I only want you to have your season, for which you have worked so hard! Ten thousand crowns is a fortune that will permit you to redeem Madame Goldentrill's performances, which will sell out, with artistic productions of obscure masterpieces that no one wants to hear!.

**Scruples:**     But my principles! My ideals! My reputation! Let me go to my farm before she arrives!

**Bluff:**     You would only collide with her on the stairs! *(He forcibly restrains Scruples.)* No, Mr. Scruples, it is the purpose to which money is put, not its source, which is important. Are churches not built with the offerings of sinners?

**Scruples:**     Perhaps; but not all sinners are singers!

*(The door flies open to permit the grand entrance of Madame Goldentrill, an authentic prima donna. She is followed by Angel who carries her impedimenta. She speaks with a marked Slavic accent.)*

## Scene 4

*(Scruples, Bluff, Angel, and Goldentrill)*

**Goldentrill:** Naughty, naughty, naughty boy! I know you have been in Salzburg at least six months and you never came to call!

**Scruples:** Forgive me, my dear lady, but the . . . (*Kisses her hand*)

**Angel:** My dear, you must not hold it against our good friend Scruples, who has been incredibly busy arranging all the conflicting details of a brilliant season.

**Bluff:** What Mr. Scruples means, Madame, is that he has been on the point of paying you a visit, at least a hundred times! Why only yesterday he was wondering if it might not be possible to induce you to lend luster to our season. . . .

**Goldentrill:** I'm sure he was! We've always been such friends! And who are you, may I ask?

**Scruples:** Permit me to present my assistant and colleague: Mr. Bluff, Madame.

**Goldentrill:** Your assistant? And colleague? How nice! Such an intelligent expression!

**Bluff:** Oh, thank you, Madame! May I have your autograph?

**Goldentrill:** But, of course! There! Now, my dear Director, I will sing for you. I want you to hear how my voice has developed in the the upper register, without losing one of those dark, lustrous, pear-shaped tones for which my lower range is so famous!

**Scruples:** I could not dream of asking an artist of your reputation to audition, Madame!

**Goldentrill:** Nonsense! Are we not all professionals? I insist! Just make yourselves comfortable, and I promise you will be amazed!

# No. 1. Ariette

**Madame Goldentrill**

My love and I are part - ed By Fate's re - lent-less rig - or, Which hound - ed our joy with cru - el vig - or! And I lie bro - ken heart - ed, Con -

Da schlägt die Ab - schieds - stun - de, um grau - sam uns zu tren - nen, um grau - sam, um grau - sam uns zu tren - nen. Wie werd' ich le - ben kön - nen, o

demned to weep and grieve all a - lone?!
Da - mon, oh - ne dich, oh - ne dich?

Through grief all too re - al,
Ich will dich be - glei - ten, *dolce*

My heart will be
im Geist dir zur

le - al; True to the love
Sei - ten schwe - ben um dich,

I once have known!
schwe - ben um dich.

But you?
Und du,

Yes
und

**Allegro moderato**

flow!
sein.

Two hearts once bound by deep af-
Ein Herz, das so der Ab - schied

fec - tion, In spite of all that fate__ has done, Will al - - ways beat as
krän-ket, dem ist kein Wan - kel - mut__ be-kannt, kein Wan - - kel - mut be-

one!
kannt!

We mock at grief, we scorn de - jec - tion;
wo - hin es auch das Schick - sal len - ket,

The blows of Fate we can de - spise, For none_____
nichts trennt das fest - ge - knüpf - te Band, nichts trennt_____

can    loose,    or break    the ties
das    fest - ge-knüpf -    te    Band,

Which hold_ us fast_ and ex - or-cise_ The e - vil pow-er    that
nichts trennt das fest - ge-knüpf - te Band,    das fest-ge - knüpf - te_

tries
Band,

## Scene 5

*(Scruples, Bluff, Angel, and Goldentrill)*

**Goldentrill:** *(After concluding her song.)* There, Mr. Scruples, I told you you'd be amazed!

**Scruples:** Madame, words fail me!

**Angel:** As usual, you were unapproachable, my dear!

**Bluff:** *What* a voice? *What* a musician! *What* art!

**Goldentrill:** Why, Mr. Bluff, now nice! I see you are a connoisseur! Now, Mr. Scruples, you have heard what I can do; as my contribution to your success in Salzburg, I am prepared to accept all the dramatic leads and be content with a mere pittance: 500 crowns per week.

**Scruples:** 500 crowns! Madame! My circumstances . . .

**Bluff:** *(Aside.)* Please, Mr. Scruples! It's Mr. Angel's money!

**Scruples:** *(Aside.)* But I wouldn't pay 500 crowns, even for the great castrato Farinelli!

**Bluff:** What Mr. Scruples means, Madame, is that he can hardly bear to think of money in connection with such art as yours!

**Goldentrill:** My dear Director, the delicacy of your sentiments more than makes up for the modesty of your offer! I shall be happy to appear as Prima Donna Assoluta of your distinguished company; you are a shrewd bargainer!

**Angel:** Yes, yes, of course! Now, my dear, if you will just wait for me in your carriage, I shall quickly draw up the contract with Mr. Scruples, then perhaps he and Mr. Bluff will join us for a little celebration?

**Bluff:** Indeed, Madame, artists should not be bothered with dull business details.

**Scruples:** But, what is there to discuss? Or celebrate?

**Goldentrill:** These gentlemen are quite right, Mr. Scruples; I find business discussions too sordid for words! I hope you won't be too long, so I shall just say: Au revoir!

*(She makes a sweeping exit through the door which is obsequiously held open by the bowing Bluff.)*

## Scene 6

*(Scruples, Bluff and Angel.)*

**Angel:** My dear Scruples, what a difference this is going to make in my life!

**Scruples:** And in mine!

**Angel:** You have been so understanding, and so helpful, that I am emboldened to ask another favor!

**Bluff:** Mr. Scruples is only too anxious to be of service, Mr. Angel! You must speak quite freely! Do!

**Angel:** Thank you; I shall. It so happens, though, for the life of me, I can't imagine how it came about, that I have a protégée; a very young lady who has not yet appeared on the stage, but who possesses the most remarkable aptitudes.

**Scruples:** Do you mean to say that you are . . . hm . . . associating with two singers at once? I would think one was enough!

**Bluff:** Oh, Mr. Scruples, Mr. Angel is a true patron of the arts!

**Angel:** Let us put it this way: I am as fascinated by Madame Goldentrill's past as I am by Miss Silverpeal's future!

**Scruples:** And they both appear to have a distinct bearing on my immediate present!

**Angel:** My dear Scruples, you are the soul of tactful wit; and, now that you have strengthened my position with Madame Goldentrill, you would make very happy by doing as much for me with Miss Silverpeal.

**Scruples:** Why don't you just build a theater of your own?

**Bluff:** What Mr. Scruples means, Mr. Angel, is that expenses have a way of leaping right over the moon when an Impresario has to make provisions for two stars in the same company.

**Angel:** Mr. Bluff, just what is your function in this company? You sound to me like the prompter! Ha, ha, ha! You must allow me my little joke! Of course you are quite right; the same holds true in my relations with the two ladies. I understand this so clearly that I am prepared to advance a further fifteen thousand crowns.

**Bluff:** Advance, Mr. Angel?

| | |
|---|---|
| **Angel:** | I mean, donate; what could I be thinking of? |
| **Scruples:** | Do I understand you correctly, Mr. Angel? You mean that you are willing to pay twenty-five thousand crowns to guarantee the engagements of these two ladies? |
| **Angel:** | Precisely, my dear Scruples. And you can keep any profits; mine will come from cheating my heirs and the tax collectors! |
| **Scruples:** | But surely there must be other conditions attached to such a princely offer? |
| **Angel:** | My dear fellow, you have me all wrong! I only want to help! I believe the people are entitled to opera and it is up to persons like myself to see that they get it! |
| **Bluff:** | There! You see, Mr. Scruples? |
| **Angel:** | Of course I shall expect a modest voice in the general policy of the theater. |
| **Scruples:** | There! You see, Mr. Bluff? |
| **Angel:** | I have always wanted to be an Impresario and you will find that I have splendid ideas about repertory, opera in the vernacular. staging, casting, conducting, promotion, ticket sales, and cultural showmanship. |
| **Scruples:** | I would never have suspected it, Mr. Angel. |
| **Angel:** | The business basis is my specialty; we financiers know a good deal about such things, believe me. It is true that I have no time to bother with art and music, but I understand merchandising and what the people want! |
| **Scruples:** | In that case, you obviously know much more than I do. |
| **Angel:** | Oh, I wouldn't say *that*, my dear Director! But to get back to Miss Silverpeal; she is waiting downstairs in the carriage and I would like to bring her up so you can judge for yourself if I have an eye for talent. |
| **Scruples:** | She is sitting with Madame Goldentrill? Congratulations! You are either a Turk, or else a born Impresario who could certainly give us all lessons! |
| **Angel:** | Don't be silly, my dear chap, of course not. They each have their own carriage and their own everything else besides. Now you can understand why I was so quick to grasp the point about the double expense! I will be right back. |
| | (*Angel exits briskly; Bluff is delighted and poor Scruples is too bewildered to even protest.*) |

## Scene 7

*(Scruples and Bluff.)*

**Bluff:** Mr. Scruples, you must admit that our prospects look considerably brighter! An hour ago we had no money at all and now, we not only have twenty-five thousand crowns, but plenty more where that came from!

**Scruples:** True, but it only makes my farm seem more attractive! This whole enterprise is looking less and less like an Opera company, and more and more like a . . .

**Bluff:** Now, now, Mr. Scruples; don't say it!

**Scruples:** I suppose with all those crowns flying about, you will want a raise? Not that I blame you . . .

**Bluff:** Oh, as your right-hand man I could do very well for myself indeed; there are so many sources of revenue which are readily available to a man in my position! However, they are not perhaps entirely ethical, and I would be reluctant to take advantage of them, particularly if you could see your way clear to augmenting my income by assigning me some suitable roles, at modest fees?

**Scruples:** My poor Bluff! That would be the greatest fraud of all! What a pair we are! You haven't the nerve to carry out your bluffs and I seem to have lost the courage of my scruples!

*(The door opens to admit Mr. Angel and the very young and beautiful spitfire, Miss Silverpeal.)*

## Scene 8

*(Scruples, Bluff, Angel and Silverpeal.)*

**Angel:** Gentlemen, here is Miss Silverpeal! And let me assure you that her voice matches her form! Can I say more?!

**Silverpeal:** If I may say so, gentlemen, Mr. Angel does not exaggerate, as you can plainly see, and as you shall clearly hear!

**Bluff:** What presence! What temperament! What looks!

**Scruples:** And what refreshing modesty!

# No. 2. Rondo

heart has but one plea-sure: Find-ing fa - vor in\_\_\_ your\_\_ sight; Since your
dei - nen hol - den Blik-ken ich mein Glück ent - dek - ken\_\_ kann, ich mein

joy is my de - light. But a - lack! The fond-est
Glück ent - dek - ken kann. A - ber ach! wenn düs-tres

rap-ture Some-times dims and fades a - way! Though we
Lei - den uns-rer Lie - be fol - gen soll, uns - rer

tire of love's sweet play,_____ Though its bliss we can't re-
Lie - be fol - gen soll,_____ loh - nen dies der Lie - be

love, my dear-est treas-ure, How I long to hold__ you__
Jüng-ling! mit Ent - zük-ken nehm' ich dei - ne Lie - be__

tight! And my heart__ has but one plea - sure: Find - ing
an, da in dei - nen hol - den Blik - ken ich mein

fa - vour in____ your__ sight; Since your joy is my de - light!
Glück ent - dek - ken____ kann, ich mein Glück ent - dek - ken

light! Scru-ples we will leave be-
kann. Nichts ist mir so__ wert und

Let our pres - ent joys suf -
geb' ich dir mein Herz zum

fice, Fu - ture woes can pay the price of par - a -
Pfand, geb' ich dir mein Herz zum Pfand, mein Herz zum

dise!
Pfand.

## Scene 9

*(Scruples, Bluff, Angel, and Silverpeal.)*

*(Miss Silverpeal concludes her song and looks for enthusiastic applause.  Bluff obliges.)*

**Angel:** Brava!  Brava!  Didn't I tell you?  Isn't she wonderful!

**Bluff:** Marvelous!  Perfect!  What eyes!  What lips!  What . . .

**Angel:** Mr. Bluff!  I will thank you to confine your enthusiasm to those details which fall within your proper professional province!

**Bluff:** I meant no offense, Mr. Angel!  I was carried away!

**Scruples:** I confess, Mr. Angel, I was most favorably impressed.  Miss Silverpeal, in spite of your lack of previous experience, I am prepared to offer you a contract; I will assign you smaller roles to begin with and will pay you two hundred and fifty crowns a week.

**Silverpeal:** Two hundred and fifty crowns a week!  I have never been so insulted!  Those are scullery maid's wages!

**Scruples:** My compliments, Mr. Angel; your kitchens must be sumptuous!

**Silverpeal:** I know my worth and I refuse to be cheated by unscrupulous Impresarios!  If you want me in your company, you will have to give the the comedy leads *and* seven hundred and fifty crowns a week *and* a backstage maid!

**Scruples:** In that case, let me . . .

**Angel:** What Mr. Scruples means, my dear, . . . Good Heavens!  Now I'm doing it too!  I mean to say, my love, that, though it's most unusual, I shall try to persuade my good friend, Mr. Scruples, to give you all the comedy leads this season *and* seven hundred and fifty crowns a week, but I'll provide the maid . . . .

*(Madame Goldentrill has entered in time to hear this, and the volcano erupts.)*

## Scene 10

*(Scruples, Bluff, Angel, Silverpeal, and Goldentrill.)*

**Goldentrill:** So you'll provide the maid?!  Charming!!!  That's why I was to wait downstairs while you arranged for this little t . . . t . . . turnip to get more than was offered to me???!!!

**Bluff:**     Madame! Pray, compose yourself! It is quite simple!

**Angel:**     Yes, my dear, I can explain everything! I was just settling the terms of your contract with Mr. Scruples when this young lady arrived to audition for soubrette parts. As he values my judgment, Mr. Scruples begged me to stay and give him my opinion. That's all there was to it, isn't that so, my dear Scruples?

**Scruples:**     Mr. Angel, do you happen to know whether music can stimulate chickens to lay more eggs?

**Angel:**     Really, my dear fellow! What are you talking about?

**Scruples:**     The most progressive farmers seem to agree that music has a most favorable effect on a cow's production of milk, so I was wondering whether the same might not be true of chickens? Eggs, not milk, of course.

**Goldentrill:**     Speaking about chickens, you haven't explained about the seven hundred and fifty crowns a week? I'm waiting!

**Angel:**     My dear, it's perfectly obvious! I only backed up this young lady's demands so I could then get your fee raised in proportion!

**Goldentrill:**     Mr. Scruples, I always understood you knew your business; Do I have to point out to you that this amateur has no experience, no technique and no method?

# No. 3. Trio

soul,
ja,

And breath con - trol!
nach ih - rem Sinn.

I've had the
Das sol - len

But plain - ly___ not_ in voice pro-
Ich will es___ ih _ nen nicht be-

ver - y best in - struc - tion!
sie mir nicht be - strei - ten!

38

43108

fear of con - tra - dic - tion: She is the worst I've ev - er
ha - be ih - res - glei - chen noch nie ge - hört und nie ge -

heard!
sehn.

**Mr. Angel** (*to Madame Goldentrill*)

Pray, calm your - self! Ig - nore her coarse-ness, You're so sus -
Was wol - len sie sich erst ent - rüs - ten, mit ein - em

cep - ti - ble to hoarse-ness! Youth lacks fi - nesse, yet
lee - ren Vor - zug brüs - ten? Ein je - des hat be -
f
p
cresc.
Madame Goldentrill
Her dic - tion must be an af -
Ge - wiss ich ha - be ih - res -
Miss Silverpeal
My dic - tion caus - es no con - stric - tion, None
Ich bin von kei - ner zu er - rei - chen, nein!
must be heard! Pray, calm your - self, Ig - nore her
son - dern Wert. Was wol - len sie sich erst ent -
tr
f p
f p

flic - tion, Which by some crime I __ have in - curred! I have no fear __
glei - chen noch nie ge - hört und nie ge - sehn, ge-wiss ich ha

I still sing free-ly as a bird; How's it done? Why thanks to
das wird mir je - des zu - ge - stehn, zu - ge - stehn, ich bin von

coarse-ness; You're so sus - cep - ti - ble to hoarse-ness! I wish to
rüs - ten, mit ei-nem lee - ren Vor-zug brü - sten, was wol - len

__ of con-tra-dic - tion: She's quite the worst __ I've ev - er heard!
be ih-res-glei - chen noch nie ge - hört __ und nie ge-sehn,

my __ ex-qui-site dic - tion Which gives the val - ue to each
kei - ner zu er - rei - chen, das wird mir je __ der zu-ge-

ven - ture a pre-dic - tion, Which if cor - rect, __ will end all
sie __ sich erst ent - rü - sten, mit ei - nem lee - ren Vor-zug

-- -- -- gro, al - le - gris - si - mo, al - le - gro, al - le -

*cresc.* *f*

gris - si - mo!

Mr. Angel

Andante

Pian, pia - no, pia - nis - si - mo, pia - nis - sis - si - mo! When

Kein

*p*

art - ists stoop to rude dis - sen - sion    They harm the art they should pro -

Künst - ler muss den an - dern ta - deln,    es setzt die Kunst zu sehr her -

*p*

3   3   3

pect That she should treat me with re - spect!
ab, ich steh' von mei ner Ford' rung ab.

tect; And that ex - plains why I ob - ject!
ab, ich ste - he e - ben falls nun ab.

men-tion? No! Such con-duct is most in-cor-rect! I know the best in -
ta deln, nein, es setzt die Kunst zu sehr her - ab. Kein Künst-ler muss je

*f p*

(You rank be - gin - ner!)
Ich bin die er - ste!

ten - tion Can of - ten have the worst ef -
ta deln, es setzt die Kunst zu sehr her -

spect! (Though en - er - get - ic, you're a com - mon en - ter -
ab, ich bin von kei - ner, bin von kei - ner zu er -

all she has I can de -
ste - he e - ben - falls nun

tect And should not
ab, es setzt, es

tain - er!)
rei - chen.

tect. (You're just pa - thet - ic, Just a bro - ken down cam -
ab, ich bin von kei - ner, bin von kei - ner zu er

be al - lowed to go un -
setzt die Kunst zu sehr her -

*(The Trio concludes, with Angel and Bluff trying to keep Golden-trill and her rival, Silverpeal, apart. Scruples pays very little attention to all the excitement. He is occupied with his own thoughts.)*

## Scene 11

*(Scruples, Bluff, Angel, Silverpeal, and Goldentrill.)*

**Angel:** Well. Mr. Scruples, what do you say to my handling of that discussion?

**Scruples:** Frankly, Mr. Angel, I paid very little attention; the truth is that the entire squabble filled me with an overwhelming nostalgia for my peaceful barnyard!

**Goldentrill:** I settled who is the prima donna of this company! Did you notice my staccato F, my sustained high E flat?

**Silverpeal:** Flat, yes! High E? Never! I don't know who you are, or what you are doing here, but I am the leading comedienne of this company and I am being paid no less than seven hundred and fifty crowns a week!

**Goldentrill:** Well, let me tell you that I am the leading tragedienne and I am being paid more than you, whatever it is, or whoever you are! I am THE Madame Goldentrill!

**Silverpeal:** Never heard of her; obviously before my time!
*(Bluff steps between them as they fly at each other.)*

**Bluff:** Ladies! Ladies! Ladies! Your hats!

**Angel:** Why don't we settle this little argument on a business basis? Why not pay both ladies one thousand crowns a week, give them star billing and agree to print their names in larger type than those of the authors and the composers combined?

**Goldentrill:** Larger than the conductors! And all the tragic leads!

**Silverpeal:** Larger than the directors! And all the comic leads!

**Angel:** That settles it! All we need do now is sign the contract! What do you say to my methods, my dear Director?

**Scruples:** I must confess that they get a certain type of result. But before we sign any contracts, I wish to make an announcement: I am doing what I have dreamed of doing for years; I am resigning my position as Impresario of this, or of any other company.

**All:** You're joking!

**Scruples:** Not at all; I am retiring to my farm in the country where I shall produce nothing but a series of tranquil Pastorales.

**All:** No! You would desert us? Leave us in the lurch?

**Scruples:** By no means; I hereby appoint my trusted colleague of many years, Mr. Bluff, as my successor.

**Bluff:** Mr. Scruples, I am deeply grateful for your confidence, but all this has convinced me that I will be happier on the stage than I could ever be in the administrative offices, at least until I retire as a singer.

**Scruples:** I was afraid of that!

**Bluff:** So, my first act as Impresario is to engage myself as leading buffo-baritone for the new season. My last act is to appoint Mr. Angel as the next Impresario, effective immediately!

**Scruples:** I knew my confidence in you was not mistaken! Bravo!

**Angel:** Of course, this takes me quite by surprise. But, to a business man, opera presents no real problems. Once I have the company on a business basis, I should be able to run it easily in my spare time.

**Silverpeal:** Mr. Scruples, we are going to miss your broad experience!

**Scruples:** Miss Silverpeal, you are best proof that experience is superfluous!

**Goldentrill:** What will happen to art and music when men like you are gone? Opera needs you, Mr. Scruples!

**Scruples:** Do not worry about art or music, Madame. They have endured for centuries, generally in spite of, not because of, individuals. Opera will again, as in the past, have good and bad Impresarios; but quacks can not destroy medicine, any more than false prophets can discredit religion. Opera, Madame, occasionally loses skirmishes, but it invariably wins the battle for survival. And so, my friends, I bid you a very good day and I wish you the success you so richly deserve.

*(Scruples exits with a sweeping bow, in utter silence.)*

## Scene 12

*(Bluff, Angel, Silverpeal, and Goldentrill.)*

**Angel:** Hmm . . . Hmm! My dear colleagues, we will strive to maintain those high standards to which my distinguished, though not immediate, predecessor dedicated his life!

**Bluff:** Hear! Hear!

**Angel:** However, from this moment on, I shall tolerate no infractions of the most business-like discipline. No one took Mr. Scruples' repeated threats of retirement seriously; but let me point out that, should I retire, my backing will accompany me, and where will you be then?

**Bluff:** Mr. General Manager, permit me to be the first to assure you of my whole-hearted cooperation. I shall be content with whatever roles you assign to me and I feel confident you will find my managerial advice invaluable!

**Silverpeal:** Mr. Angel, I agree with Mr. Bluff. I am quite prepared to undertake such lesser parts as my inexperience may dictate. With full salary and top billing, of course!

**Goldentrill:** I assume no one would dream of asking me to sing minor roles; however, I am perfectly willing to limit myself to two farewell appearances this year. Naturally, with a thousand crowns a week and star status for the whole season!

**Angel:** It is truly inspiring how putting art on a business basis harmonises the most discordant conflicts!

**Bluff:** Let us toast the indispensable man: the Impresario, whoever he may be!

**Goldentrill:** Past!

**Angel:** Present!

**Silverpeal:** And future!

**All:** The Impresario!

# No. 4. Finale

68

tall, Yet can make an art - ist small?
klein, macht den gröss - ten Künst - ler klein.

tall, Yet can make an art - ist small?
klein, macht den gröss - ten Künst - ler klein.

tall, Yet can make an art - ist small?
klein, macht den gröss - ten Künst - ler klein.

Mr. Angel

Op - 'ra on a busi - ness ba - sis Is a thing I—mean to
Ei - nig - keit rühm' ich vor al - len an - dern Tu gen - den uns

test,— I will find some fresh new fa - ces, So the pub - lic's not de -
an,— denn das Gan - ze— muss ge - fal - len, und nicht bloss ein einz'l - ner

43108

Madame Goldentrill

I ad - vise com - plete sub - mis - sion Since our backs are to the—
Künst - ler müs - sen frei - lich stre - ben stets des Vor - zugs wert zu—

Miss Silverpeal

I ad - vise com - plete sub - mis - sion Since our backs are to the—
Künst - ler müs - sen frei - lich stre - ben stets des Vor - zugs wert zu—

I ad - vise com - plete sub - mis - sion Since your backs are to the—
Künst - ler müs - sen frei - lich stre - ben stets des Vor - zugs wert zu—

wall! Treat each one with deep sus - pi - cion, Play the
sein, doch sich selbst den Vor - zug ge - ben ü - ber

wall! Treat each one with deep sus - pi - cion, Play the
sein, doch sich selbst den Vor - zug ge - ben ü - ber

wall! Treat each one with deep sus - pi - cion, Play the
sein, doch sich selbst den Vor - zug ge - ben ü - ber

Ev - 'ry art - ist has a mis - sion, Though his pub - lic may be—
Künst - ler müs - sen frei - lich stre - ben stets des Vor - zugs wert zu—

Ev - 'ry art - ist has a mis - sion, Though his pub - lic may be—
Künst - ler müs - sen frei - lich stre - ben stets des Vor - zugs wert zu—

Ev - 'ry art - ist has a mis - sion, Though his pub - lic may be—
Künst - ler müs - sen frei - lich stre - ben stets des Vor - zugs wert zu—

small; In the case of a mu - si - cian, He must serve the com - po -
sein, doch sich selbst den Vor - zug ge - ben, ü - ber and - re sich er -

small; In the case of a mu - si - cian, He must serve the com - po -
sein, doch sich selbst den Vor - zug ge - ben, ü - ber and - re sich er -

small; In the case of a mu - si - cian, He must serve the com - po -
sein, doch sich selbst den Vor - zug ge - ben, ü - ber and - re sich er -

round And that, like mine, your meth-od's sound! Bluff is a
klar, der er - ste Buf - fo, das ist klar. Ich hei - sse

name! Des - tined to fame, And great ac -
Buff, ich hei - sse Buff; nur um ein

claim! My life will be one long o - va - tion!You'll nev - er see this Bluff
O brauch ich den Na - men zu ver - lan-gern, so heiss ich oh - ne Streit,

bluff - ing! That was "D" yet I'm scarce-ly puf - fing!
Buf - fo, er - go bin ich der er - ste Buf - fo,

78

43108

Curtain